Planet Earth
Crosswords

Phil Clarke

Illustrated by the Pope Twins

Designed by Michael Hill

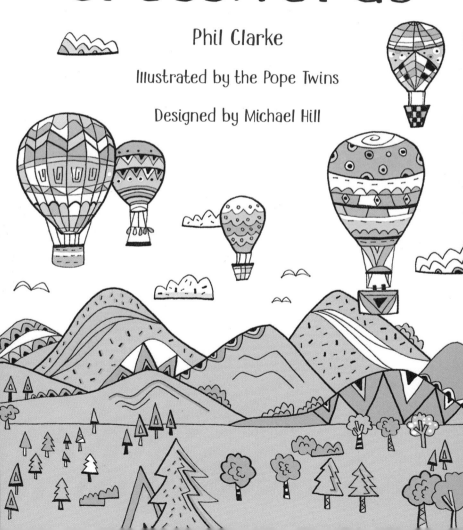

How to solve crosswords

The crosswords in this book start simple and gradually get harder. If you're new to crosswords, here are a few tips.

It's a good idea to use a pencil with an eraser or to write lightly with a pen so that you can remove or write over mistakes.

There are two lists of clues: one for answers that read across the crossword grid, and one for those that read down. Some answers are split into an across and a down part.

Start wherever you like. If you can't solve one clue, move onto another that crosses it. The letters from that answer will help you. For example, solving the down answers below gives you G_E_T for 4 across, leading you towards the answer: GREET

ACROSS

1. Instruction to go to the next page (1.1.1.)
4. Say hello (5)
5. Bite (3)

DOWN

1. Hogs, swine (4)
2. Salty water separating continents (5)
3. Move a foot forward (4)

¹P	T	²O		
I		C		³S
⁴G		E		T
S		A		E
		⁵N	I	P

After each clue you can see how many letters the answer has, and whether it contains one word or more.

If you get stuck, or your answers don't seem to fit, you can check all the answers at the back of the book.

Happy puzzling!

ACROSS

1. It covers two-thirds of the Earth (5)
4. The path of a moon or space station as it circles a planet (5)
5. The Earth spins from west to ____ (4)

DOWN

1. Used a pen to make letters (5)
2. Pipes (5)
3. Large rodents (4)

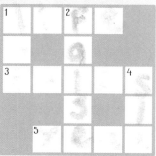

ACROSS

1. Planet Earth is the only place that this definitely exists (4)
3. Earth's extreme northern and southern points (5)
5. How long it takes the Earth to travel around the Sun (4)

DOWN

1. Drink water like a dog (3)
2. Opposite of true (5)
4. Title for a knight (3)

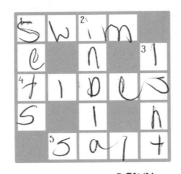

Crossword grid:

S	W	I	M	
E		N		I
T	I	D	E	S
S		I		N
	S	A	L	T

ACROSS

1. Move yourself through water (4)
4. The sea's high and low _ _ _ _ _ are when it comes in and goes out (5)
5. Seawater tastes of this (4)

DOWN

1. The Sun _ _ _ _ in the west (4)
2. Large South Asian country (5)
3. Short for "is not" (4)

Crossword grid:

R	E	D
O		I
W	A	V	E	S
		E		A
		R	O	D

ACROSS

1. The _ _ _ Sea separates North Africa from Arabia (3)
3. Ripples and crests of the sea (5)
5. Fisherman's tool (3)

DOWN

1. Use oars (3)
2. Undersea explorer (5)
4. Unhappy (3)

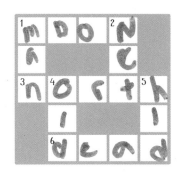

5

ACROSS

1. It orbits the Earth (4)
3. The _ _ _ _ _ Sea lies between Great Britain and Scandinavia (5)
6. The _ _ _ _ Sea between Israel and Jordan got its name because it is so salty that nothing can live in it (4)

DOWN

1. Adult male (3)
2. It's used to catch lots of fish at once (3)
4. Opposite of young (3)
5. Concealed itself (3)

6

ACROSS

1. The _ _ _ _ _ Sea, north of Turkey, was named for its sudden, dark storms (5)
4. Stay at the water's surface (5)
5. Took a seat (3)

DOWN

2. Calms (5)
3. Shoreline (5)

7

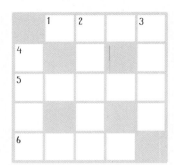

ACROSS

1. Hong ____, big port city in South China (4)
5. Ascend (5)
6. Lots (4)

DOWN

2. The star pattern of the Hunter (5)
3. The ____ Desert lies between North China and Mongolia (4)
4. Con, fraud (4)

8

ACROSS

2. Board game with kings and queens (5)
4. Test, court case (5)

DOWN

1. Start (5)
2. Large town (4)
3. Glossy natural fabric first made in China (4)

9

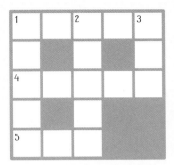

ACROSS

1. An oyster's treasure (5)
4. Very pleased with yourself or someone else (5)
5. China's flag is _ _ _ with yellow stars (3)

DOWN

1. This Chinese invention is used for writing on (5)
2. Deliberately miss (5)
3. Boy, young man (3)

10

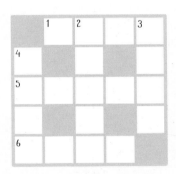

ACROSS

1. The Great _ _ _ _ of China stretches across much of its northern border (4)
5. The tops of buildings (5)
6. New _ _ _ _ is China's biggest festival (4)

DOWN

2. Scent (5)
3. Final (4)
4. The Terracotta _ _ _ _ guards the tomb of China's First Emperor (4)

11

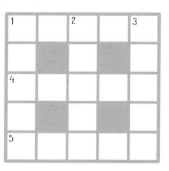

ACROSS

1. Largest of the Greek islands (5)
4. Rome is the capital of which country? (5)
5. Alexander the _ _ _ _ _ was a king of Ancient Macedonia who conquered many countries (5)

DOWN

1. Hold on tightly (5)
2. Avoid a pursuer (5)
3. Land of the Pyramids (5)

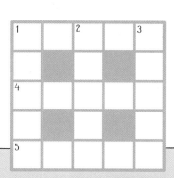

ACROSS

1. Country in Southern Europe, capital Madrid (5)
4. Island near Naples, Italy (5)
5. It grows into a plant (4)

DOWN

1. A vacuum cleaner _ _ _ _ _ up dirt (5)
2. Crunchy fruit (5)
3. You hit it with a hammer (4)

ACROSS

1. Big city in northern Italy famous for its fashion and soccer teams (5)
4. North African country south of Italy, capital Tripoli (5)
5. Book of maps (5)

DOWN

1. Little island-nation south of Sicily, capital Valletta (5)
2. Information sticker (5)
3. Approaches (5)

14

ACROSS

1. Riverside (4)
3. Go with the flow (5)
5. Kink, curve (4)

DOWN

1. River bottom (3)
2. Sound (5)
4. Smidgen (3)

15

ACROSS

1. Tall riverside grasses (5)
3. The end of a river where it meets the sea (5)
6. Faith (5)

DOWN

1. Male sheep (3)
2. Little spot (3)
4. Paddle for a boat (3)
5. You wear it on your head (3)

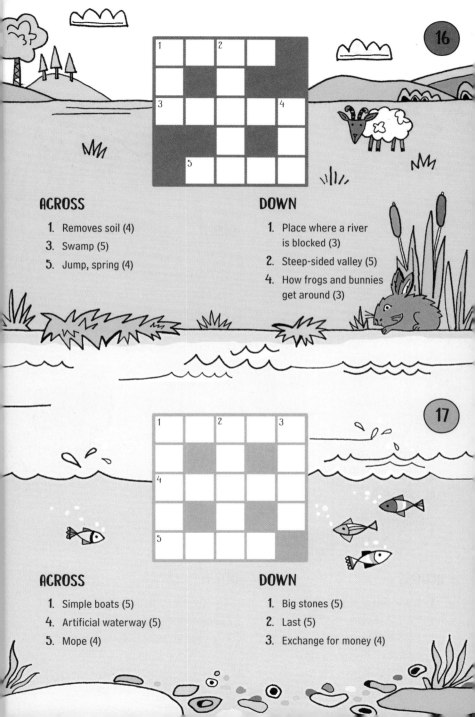

ACROSS

1. Removes soil (4)
3. Swamp (5)
5. Jump, spring (4)

DOWN

1. Place where a river is blocked (3)
2. Steep-sided valley (5)
4. How frogs and bunnies get around (3)

ACROSS

1. Simple boats (5)
4. Artificial waterway (5)
5. Mope (4)

DOWN

1. Big stones (5)
2. Last (5)
3. Exchange for money (4)

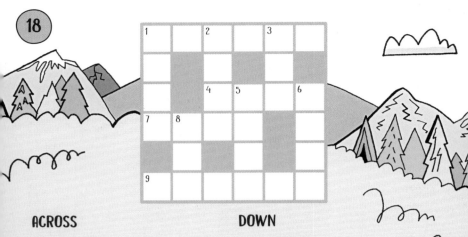

18

ACROSS

1. Fortress (6)
4. Second-hand (4)
7. Capital of Switzerland (4)
9. Czech capital (6)

DOWN

1. Baby's bed (4)
2. Opposite of sweet (4)
3. Bruce ___, martial arts expert (3)
5. Comfortable (4)
6. You roll them in board games (4)
8. Organ of hearing (3)

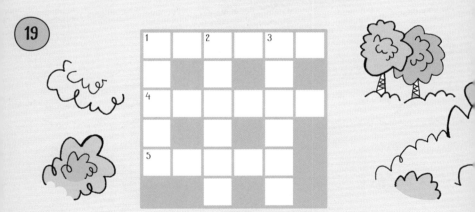

19

ACROSS

1. Great river of Europe in a famous waltz by Johann Strauss (6)
4. Narrows (6)
5. Title of a famous story about a Swiss orphan girl (5)

DOWN

1. Language of the Netherlands (5)
2. Serviette (6)
3. Capital of Germany (6)

ACROSS

1. Poland's capital (6)
4. Europe's longest mountain range (4)
6. Make money by working (4)
7. Truthful (6)

DOWN

1. Riches (6)
2. Ready to eat (4)
3. Nut with a wrinkled shell (6)
5. Out of danger (4)

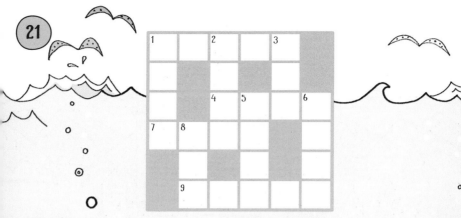

ACROSS

1. (with 2 down) Undersea ridge made up of the rocky bodies of tiny, flower-like creatures (5, 4)
4. Tips (4)
7. Married woman (4)
9. Member of a youth organization who goes camping and earns badges (5)

DOWN

1. Crab's pincer (4)
2. (see 1 across)
3. Guided (3)
5. *Finding _ _ _ _*, 2003 movie about a fish looking for his lost son (4)
6. Opposite of hard (4)
8. Short for "it is" (3)

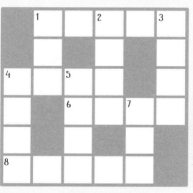

ACROSS

1. Soft-bodied, ten-legged sea creature (5)
4. It hops, and lays its eggs in ponds (4)
6. Really, extremely (4)
8. First thing in the morning (5)

DOWN

1. Polite title for an unknown man (3)
2. Strongly encourage (4)
3. *Finding _ _ _ _*, 2016 movie about a forgetful fish (4)
4. A common starfish has this many arms (4)
5. Above, on top of (4)
7. Manta _ _ _, big flat fish (3)

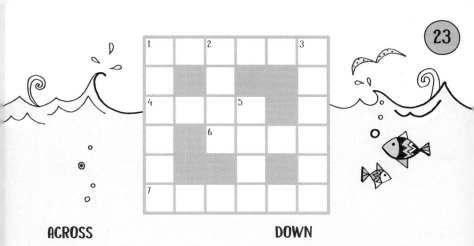

ACROSS

1. A sea _ _ _ _ _ _ is a spiny, round sea creature (6)
4. Shellfish (4)
6. Courageous (4)
7. Soft-bodied, holey sea creature (6)

DOWN

1. Your father's brothers (6)
2. Clawed sea creature (4)
3. Sewing tool (6)
5. Complain (4)

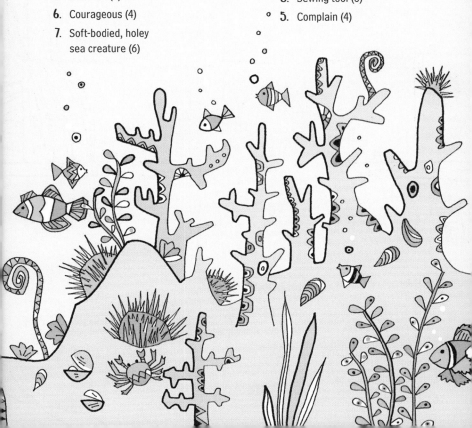

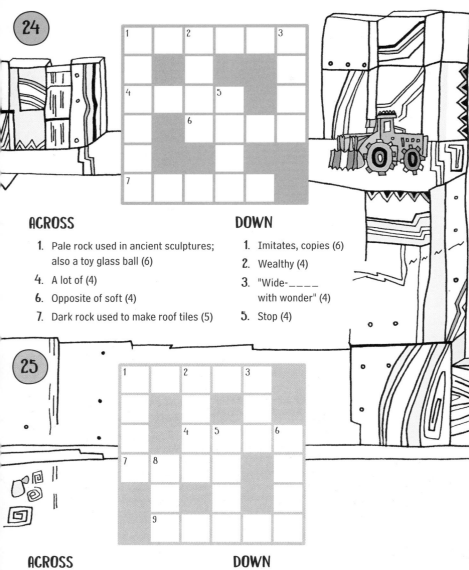

ACROSS

1. Pale rock used in ancient sculptures; also a toy glass ball (6)
4. A lot of (4)
6. Opposite of soft (4)
7. Dark rock used to make roof tiles (5)

DOWN

1. Imitates, copies (6)
2. Wealthy (4)
3. "Wide-____ with wonder" (4)
5. Stop (4)

25

ACROSS

1. Soft, crumbly white rock (5)
4. Breakout of blackheads (4)
7. Toy that goes up and down on a string (2-2)
9. Flat pieces of hard material, used to cover roofs, walls or floors (5)

DOWN

1. Sticky mud that can be easily shaped (4)
2. "An apple a day keeps the doctor ____" (4)
3. Short for Kenneth (3)
5. Black rock burned as fuel (4)
6. Consumes (4)
8. Opposite of in (3)

ACROSS

1. Hard rock crystal (6)
4. Stumble (4)
6. Move upwards (4)
7. Shouted (6)

DOWN

1. Place where rock is removed from the ground in the open air (6)
2. Tiny insects (4)
3. Sped, dashed (6)
5. Genuine (4)

ACROSS

1. Bush from Asia used to make a popular drink (3)

3. Grain, often white, eaten with Asian food (4)

5. "You can't _ _ _ _ your cake and eat it" (4)

6. "I want _ _ _ _ one, not that one" (4)

7. Long-tailed amphibian (4)

8. Unique genetic code (1.1.1.)

DOWN

1. Make fun of (5)

2. 007 is a secret _ _ _ _ _ (5)

3. Valued (5)

4. This Asian country grows the most 3 across (5)

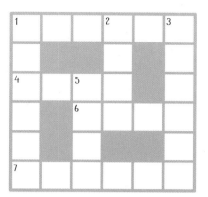

ACROSS

1. Bronzed skin (6)
4. Face disguise (4)
6. Care for, nurture (4)
7. Russia spreads across both Asia and _ _ _ _ _ _ (6)

DOWN

1. Uncomplicated (6)
2. Grab (4)
3. Asian-style pasta strip (6)
5. Mix with a spoon (4)

ACROSS

1. Big island off Eastern China (6)
5. Bound, jump (4)
7. Relax (4)
9. Roam (6)

DOWN

2. Noah's boat (3)
3. "_ _ _ _ the slate clean" (4)
4. Following, coming after (4)
5. Opposite of fast (4)
6. Middle Eastern country also known as Persia (4)
8. Short for Susan (3)

ACROSS

1. The largest and most northerly American state (6)
5. Los _ _ _ _ _ _ _, California's biggest city (7)
7. Grassy American plain (7)
10. The _ _ _ _ _ _ Gate Bridge spans the entrance to San Francisco Bay (6)

DOWN

2. Short for Leonard (3)
3. Not ordinary (7)
4. Playing card (3)
5. Program on a smartphone or tablet (3)
6. Sense with your eyes (3)
8. Old piece of cloth (3)
9. Short for I have (3)

ACROSS

1. Towering tree that grows on the coast of California (7)
5. _ _ _ _ _ _ _ Valley is the name given to an area around San Francisco Bay known for its many computer and technology firms (7)
6. Rough, imprecise (7)
7. Learn about (5)

DOWN

1. The Bering Strait separates the USA from which country? (6)
2. Least bright (7)
3. Garden full of fruit trees (7)
4. Give money to charity (6)

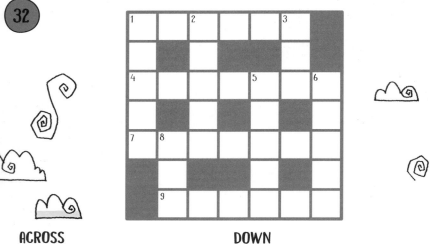

ACROSS

1. Grassy field (6)
4. Fork-tailed bird (7)
7. A _ _ _ _ _ _ _ harvester is a vehicle for gathering crops (7)
9. Opposite of remember (6)

DOWN

1. Pop or jazz, for example (5)
2. It wakes you up (5)
3. Dr. _ _ _ travels through time (3)
5. Deceiving (5)
6. Grain often ground into flour (5)
8. Opposite of on (3)

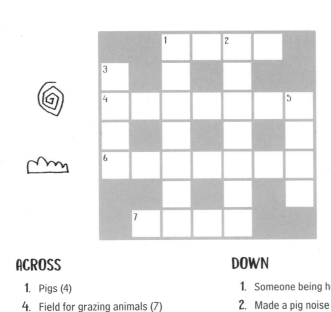

ACROSS

1. Pigs (4)
4. Field for grazing animals (7)
6. Farm vehicle used for towing (7)
7. Give food (4)

DOWN

1. Someone being held to ransom (7)
2. Made a pig noise (7)
3. Round mark (4)
5. Donkeys have long _ _ _ _ (4)

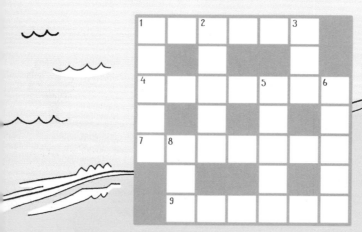

ACROSS

1. The Bay of _ _ _ _ _ _ separates India from Thailand and Malaysia (6)
4. Disgusts (7)
7. Weird (7)
9. Grand royal house (6)

DOWN

1. They have wings and feathers (5)
2. At no time (5)
3. Set on fire, ignited (3)
5. Sri _ _ _ _ _, large island country off the south coast of India (5)
6. Fine strainer (5)
8. Piece of advice (3)

35

ACROSS

1. Monkey-like animals from Madagascar (6)
4. The _ _ _ _ _ _ _ Gulf separates Iran from Arabia (7)
5. Get given (7)
7. The part of a suitcase that you grip (6)

DOWN

1. Untruth (3)
2. Guide wrongly, deceive (7)
3. Burn slightly (5)
4. Big city on the west coast of Australia named after a city in Scotland (5)
6. Compete, struggle (3)

ACROSS

2. Russia's biggest region, known for its vast pine forests and cold winters (7)
5. Bordering Russia, the _ _ _ _ _ _ _ Sea shares its name with a prince in a book by C.S. Lewis (7)
6. Sickness (7)

DOWN

1. Reach a place (6)
2. Russian city that hosted the 2014 Winter Olympics, and games in the 2018 Soccer World Cup (5)
3. St. _ _ _ _ _ _ Cathedral is in Moscow's Red Square (6)
4. Mother's sisters (5)

ACROSS

1. Russia used to be the largest country in a state named the _ _ _ _ _ _ Union (6)
5. Place of higher education (7)
6. Gazing (7)
8. Famous search engine co-created by Russian-born Sergey Brin (6)

DOWN

1. Bags like Santa's (5)
2. Russian river, Europe's longest (5)
3. The last part of the day (7)
4. The Justice _ _ _ _ _ _ is a superhero team including Superman and Wonder Woman (6)
7. Pull sharply (3)

ACROSS

1. In which North African country can you see the Sphinx, or giant statues of Pharaoh Ramesses the Great? (5)
5. Italian for ice cream (6)
6. Greece's capital, the hottest city in Europe (6)
8. The most dramatic part of something, such as a movie or sports match (6)

DOWN

2. Region of Western India famous for its golden beaches (3)
3. Capital of Arizona, one of America's hottest cities, it's named for a bird in old stories that was reborn in fire (7)
4. Small feature (6)
7. Make a musical sound with your mouth closed (3)

ACROSS

1. _ _ _ _ _ Valley in the desert of California, USA, has the record for the highest temperature ever (5)
5. Insect's feeler, or radio receiver (7)
6. Hairy strip above an eye (7)
7. Big, hot country south of Egypt (5)

DOWN

1. Sliding compartment in a desk (6)
2. They grow on a deer's head (7)
3. 20+30+50 (7)
4. Australia's hottest city, it was named after a scientist famed for his theory of evolution (6)

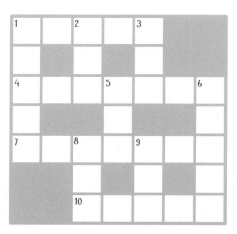

ACROSS

1. Tree that sounds like it should grow by the sea (5)
4. TV controls (7)
7. Tree mentioned in a nursery rhyme about a clock (7)
10. Tree with small, purple berries, or someone older than you (5)

DOWN

1. Tree with silvery, papery bark that peels away (5)
2. Tall, shady tree (3)
3. Strike (3)
5. Acorns grow on this tree (3)
6. More crafty (5)
8. Stick used in pool and snooker (3)
9. "As _ _ _ as the hills" (3)

ACROSS

1. Tree with scented wood and wide-spreading branches (5)
4. The juice inside a tree or plant (3)
5. Evergreen tree (3)
6. Decay (3)
7. Purpose (3)
8. Tavern (3)
9. Glue (5)

DOWN

1. Common evergreen tree (7)
2. When it is light (7)
3. Tree with red-orange berries, also known as mountain ash (5)
4. The cut-off base of a tree (5)

ACROSS

1. Passenger ship that sank off the coast of Canada in 1912 (7)
4. Speed, or charge (4)
6. Wonder, admiration (3)
8. Short for amplifier (3)
10. Snake-like fishes (4)
11. Ocean plant-life (7)

DOWN

1. Huge, speedy seafish whose meat is sold in cans (4)
2. Alexandre Dumas wrote The _ _ _ _ _ Musketeers (5)
3. Thing, especially in a list (4)
5. Liking, preference (5)
7. "Wish you _ _ _ _ here" (4)
9. Pool, often with fish (4)

ACROSS

1. _ _ _ _ _ _ Earhart, first female pilot to fly solo across the Atlantic (6)
6. "Mother shook _ _ _ head" (3)
7. Place with exercise machines (3)
8. Giant bird encountered by Sindbad the Sailor (3)
9. Seafish (3)
10. Not quickly (6)

DOWN

2. North African country, its biggest city is Casablanca (7)
3. Sensible, rational (7)
4. The Spanish _ _ _ _ _ _ was a fleet that tried to attack England in 1588 (6)
5. Sailors' maps (6)

ACROSS

1. This Japanese car company is one of the biggest in the world (6)
4. Hot, green Japanese sauce (6)
7. Traditional Japanese robe (6)
10. Protect (6)

DOWN

1. Pull a vehicle or trailer (3)
2. Opposite of no (3)
3. Extraterrestrial (5)
5. Inquired (5)
6. Point at a target (3)
8. Be in debt (3)
9. Opposite of even (3)

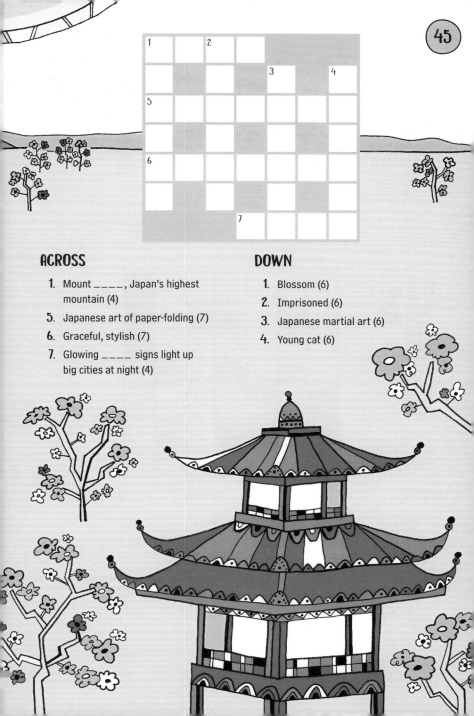

ACROSS

1. Mount _ _ _ _, Japan's highest mountain (4)
5. Japanese art of paper-folding (7)
6. Graceful, stylish (7)
7. Glowing _ _ _ _ signs light up big cities at night (4)

DOWN

1. Blossom (6)
2. Imprisoned (6)
3. Japanese martial art (6)
4. Young cat (6)

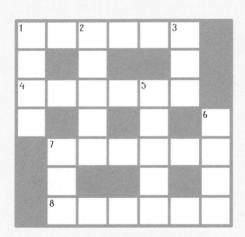

ACROSS

1. The world's biggest desert, it covers most of North Africa (6)
4. Observe (6)
7. Awkward, bungling (6)
8. Number of months in a year (6)

DOWN

1. What dunes are made of (4)
2. Place where you can pay to stay (5)
3. A gorilla, for example (3)
5. Humped desert animal (5)
6. Sort, kind (4)
7. Slice, chop (3)

ACROSS

1. Hairless (4)
3. Every one (3)
5. Shaving tool (5)
6. Body-length clothes (5)
7. You might do this to show that you agree (3)
8. This rarely falls in deserts (4)

DOWN

1. Dry and lifeless (6)
2. Long-tailed reptile (6)
3. Saudi _ _ _ _ _ _, desert country in the Middle East (6)
4. Teaching session (6)

48

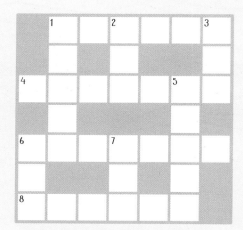

ACROSS

1. Capital of the UK (6)
4. Packed with people (7)
6. America's biggest city (3, 4)
8. Meal that combines breakfast and lunch (6)

DOWN

1. Great in size (5)
2. At this time (3)
3. To ___ off means to fall asleep (3)
5. Soil (5)
6. The end of a pen (3)
7. Currency of Japan (3)

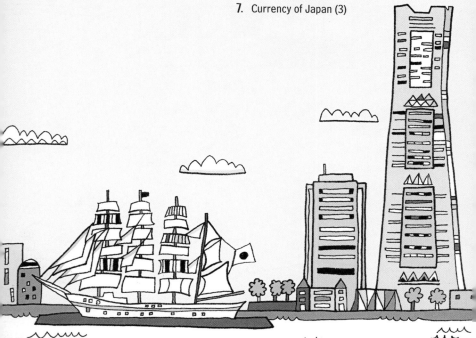

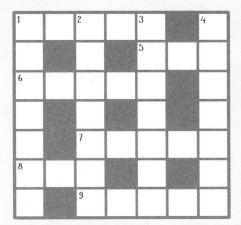

ACROSS

1. Capital of France (5)
5. Drink made from leaves (3)
6. Capital of Egypt (5)
7. Empty, featureless (5)
8. ___ de Janeiro, capital of Brazil (3)
9. Sunken ship (5)

DOWN

1. Image (7)
2. Arc of light seen in the sky on wet, sunny days (7)
3. Space for keeping things (7)
4. Capital of Thailand (7)

50

ACROSS

1. This Mexican state gives its name to a famous hot pepper sauce (7)
5. Singer from Barbados who had a huge hit with *Umbrella* (7)
6. Walking with difficulty (7)
7. Female sibling (6)

DOWN

1. Sea reptiles with shells (7)
2. English-speaking Caribbean country, capital Nassau (7)
3. Dawn (7)
4. Citrus fruit (6)

ACROSS

1. Johnny Depp starred in
   _ _ _ _ _ _ _ of the Caribbean (7)
4. Small Central American country famed
   for its big canal, and the straw hats
   that are named after it (6)
7. Cinnamon and nutmeg, for example (6)
10. Fairy-tale creature that looks
    like a fish-tailed woman (7)

DOWN

1. Burst (3)
2. Move rapidly (3)
3. Remove, rub out (5)
5. Passage between shelves or seats (5)
6. Muhammad _ _ _, US wrestler (3)
8. American spy organization (1.1.1.)
9. Glum (3)

52

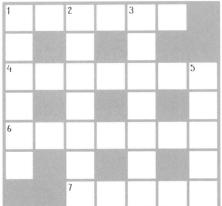

ACROSS

1. At the age of 11, in Pakistan, _ _ _ _ _ _ Yousafzai risked her life to speak out for the right of girls to be educated (6)
4. Rainy season in India (7)
6. Not appearing to get older (7)
7. Some elephants have these long teeth, used for digging and fighting (5)

DOWN

1. Big city on India's west coast, old name Bombay (6)
2. Biggest from end to end (7)
3. Untightens (7)
5. Trunks are elephants' _ _ _ _ _ (5)

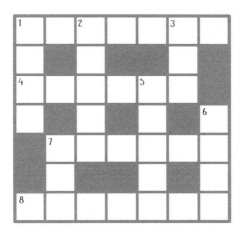

ACROSS

1. _ _ _ _ _ _ _ Gandhi was a great Indian leader (7)
4. Sacred river of India and Bangladesh (6)
7. Thick tropical forest (6)
8. Disregards (7)

DOWN

1. Tall cups with handles (4)
2. Follower of India's biggest religion (5)
3. Title a woman uses to show that she is married (3)
5. Keen (5)
6. Lower limbs (4)
7. Run slowly (3)

ACROSS

1. Animals that dig tunnels (5)
4. Deep hole (3)
6. Someone who works underground (5)
7. Opposite of outer (5)
8. Most people have this many fingers (3)
9. Catches their breath (5)

DOWN

1. Instant in time (6)
2. Giving away for a while (7)
3. Water sources that flow out of the ground (7)
5. Large prickles (6)

ACROSS

1. Thick electric wire that runs underground (5)
4. Powder left after burning (3)
6. Parts of a plant that grow underground (5)
7. Most people do this at night (5)
8. Equal score, draw (3)
9. Echo-based navigation system used by submarines (5)

DOWN

1. Orange vegetable (6)
2. Looks around casually (7)
3. Opposite of western (7)
5. Picnic basket (6)

ACROSS

1. Australian wilderness (7)
5. Rushed (7)
7. Day trips (7)
8. Sightseer (7)

DOWN

2. Big red rock in the middle of Australia, also known as Ayers Rock (5)
3. Australia's Great _ _ _ _ _ _ _ Reef is the world's largest coral reef (7)
4. Slang for child (3)
6. Borders (5)
7. Choose (3)

ACROSS

1. Tree-climbing Australian animal (5)
4. Went to see (7)
5. Does again (7)
9. A book by Roald Dahl about a schoolgirl with special powers; her name also appears in an old Australian song (7)

DOWN

1. Blade (5)
2. _ _ _ _ _ Springs, town right in the middle of Australia. It was named after a lady with the same name as a storybook heroine who visited Wonderland (5)
3. Short for are not (5)
5. Charge into (3)
6. Tame animal (3)
7. "_ _ _ that glitters is not gold" (3)
8. Australia and New Zealand are separated by the Tasman _ _ _ (3)

ACROSS

1. Snowstorm (8)
5. Roman emperor (4)
6. Box (5)
8. Working with (5)
10. Tilt (4)
11. Tornado (7)

DOWN

1. Bangle (8)
2. Thought (4)
3. Areas (5)
4. Long spell of dry weather when water supplies run low (7)
7. Melodies (5)
9. Lazy (4)

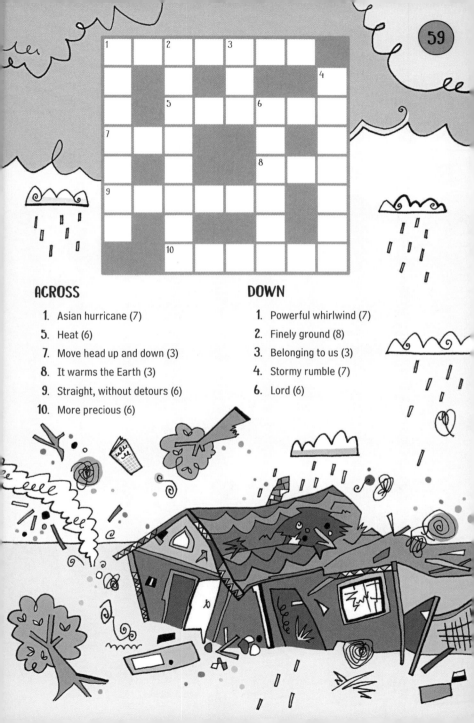

ACROSS

1. Asian hurricane (7)
5. Heat (6)
7. Move head up and down (3)
8. It warms the Earth (3)
9. Straight, without detours (6)
10. More precious (6)

DOWN

1. Powerful whirlwind (7)
2. Finely ground (8)
3. Belonging to us (3)
4. Stormy rumble (7)
6. Lord (6)

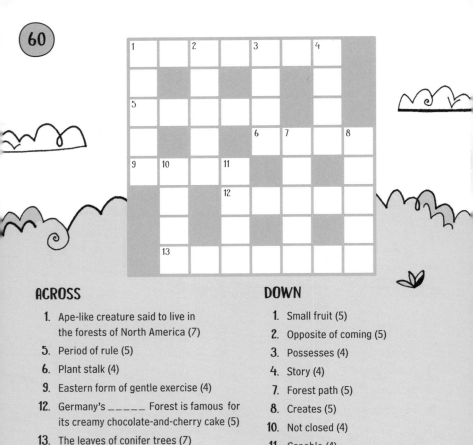

60

ACROSS

1. Ape-like creature said to live in the forests of North America (7)
5. Period of rule (5)
6. Plant stalk (4)
9. Eastern form of gentle exercise (4)
12. Germany's _ _ _ _ _ Forest is famous for its creamy chocolate-and-cherry cake (5)
13. The leaves of conifer trees (7)

DOWN

1. Small fruit (5)
2. Opposite of coming (5)
3. Possesses (4)
4. Story (4)
7. Forest path (5)
8. Creates (5)
10. Not closed (4)
11. Capable (4)

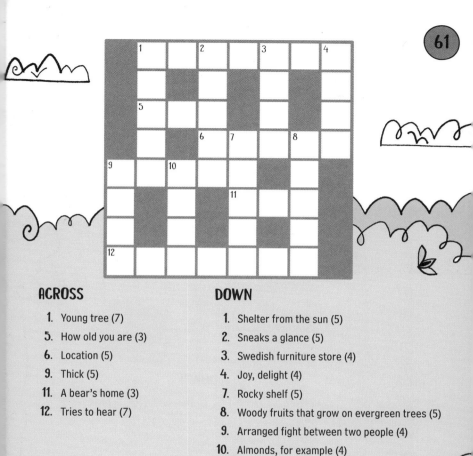

ACROSS

1. Young tree (7)
5. How old you are (3)
6. Location (5)
9. Thick (5)
11. A bear's home (3)
12. Tries to hear (7)

DOWN

1. Shelter from the sun (5)
2. Sneaks a glance (5)
3. Swedish furniture store (4)
4. Joy, delight (4)
7. Rocky shelf (5)
8. Woody fruits that grow on evergreen trees (5)
9. Arranged fight between two people (4)
10. Almonds, for example (4)

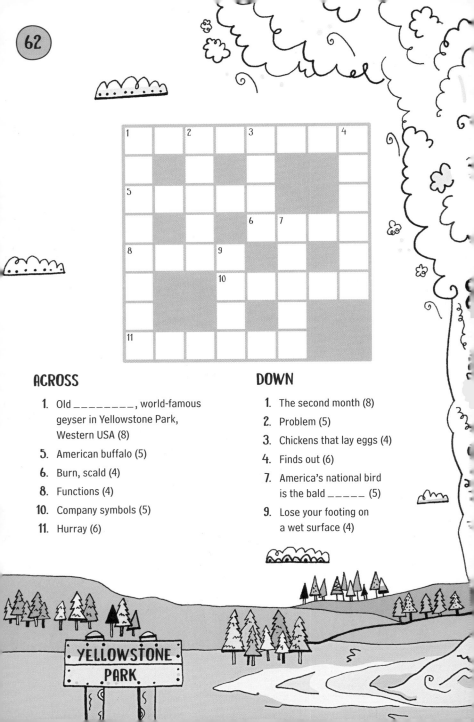

ACROSS

1. Old _ _ _ _ _ _ _ _, world-famous geyser in Yellowstone Park, Western USA (8)
5. American buffalo (5)
6. Burn, scald (4)
8. Functions (4)
10. Company symbols (5)
11. Hurray (6)

DOWN

1. The second month (8)
2. Problem (5)
3. Chickens that lay eggs (4)
4. Finds out (6)
7. America's national bird is the bald _ _ _ _ _ (5)
9. Lose your footing on a wet surface (4)

ACROSS

1. Large North American bear (7)
4. You twist it to fix it in place (5)
6. A bird lays eggs in it (4)
8. Hand out cards for a game (4)
9. Setting (5)
10. Earn admiration (7)

DOWN

1. Huge people in old legends (6)
2. Energy, gusto (4)
3. Big (5)
5. Wild, dog-like animals (6)
7. It puffs out of a boiling kettle (5)
8. Herd animals with antlers (4)

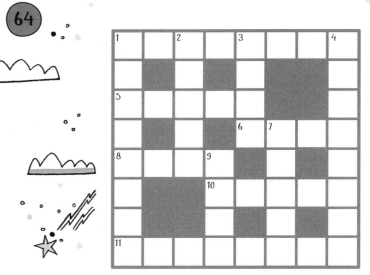

64

ACROSS

1. Most of the 4 downs are thought to have died out after an _ _ _ _ _ _ _ _ struck Central America (8)

5. *Triceratops* was named for the three _ _ _ _ _ on its face (5)

6. Admirable person, role model (4)

8. Other (4)

10. Stage play (5)

11. Person in charge of making a movie (8)

DOWN

1. Accomplished (8)

2. Changes direction (5)

3. Hasty, unwise (4)

4. Prehistoric reptile (8)

7. Precise (5)

9. Side (4)

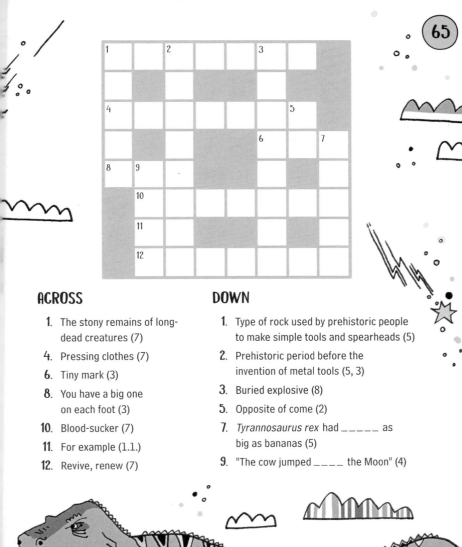

ACROSS

1. The stony remains of long-dead creatures (7)
4. Pressing clothes (7)
6. Tiny mark (3)
8. You have a big one on each foot (3)
10. Blood-sucker (7)
11. For example (1.1.)
12. Revive, renew (7)

DOWN

1. Type of rock used by prehistoric people to make simple tools and spearheads (5)
2. Prehistoric period before the invention of metal tools (5, 3)
3. Buried explosive (8)
5. Opposite of come (2)
7. *Tyrannosaurus rex* had _ _ _ _ _ as big as bananas (5)
9. "The cow jumped _ _ _ _ the Moon" (4)

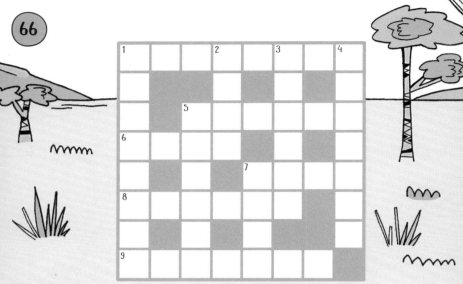

ACROSS

1. East African country, capital Addis Ababa (8)
5. Wanting something to happen (6)
6. Pleasantly cold (4)
7. 60 minutes (4)
8. The _ _ _ _ _ _ Ocean lies east of Africa (6)
9. This West African country has more people living in it than any other country in Africa (7)

DOWN

1. Time when you vote for leaders (8)
2. Hero (4)
3. Jail (6)
4. Biggest country in Africa (7)
5. Sausage served in a long roll (3, 3)
7. It grows on your head (4)

ACROSS

1. British queen who gave her name to Africa's largest lake, and waterfall (8)
5. Tries, samples (6)
7. Speed contest (4)
8. Shine gently (4)
10. Lead and copper are both what? (6)
12. Intelligent, playful sea animals (8)

DOWN

1. Animal doctor (3)
2. Tradition (6)
3. Finished (4)
4. Dull pain (4)
6. Trip to see African wildlife (6)
8. Precious metal (4)
9. Cry (4)
11. British Army Special Forces unit (1.1.1.)

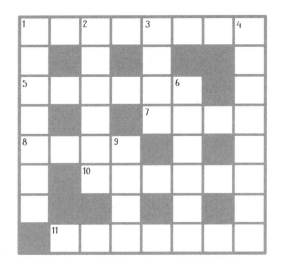

ACROSS

1. Famous volcano near Naples, Italy (8)
5. Bowl-shaped area around the opening of a volcano (6)
7. Bend out of shape (4)
8. Measurement equal to about 2.5cm (4)
10. In which US state in the Pacific is Mauna Kea, the world's tallest volcano? (6)
11. Take part in a contest (7)

DOWN

1. Those who suffer a disaster or crime (7)
2. Hunt to find something (6)
3. Outlook, vista (4)
4. Unexpected event (8)
6. Destroy, ransack (6)
9. Damage (4)

ACROSS

1. Roman city destroyed by a volcanic eruption in AD79 (7)
5. Is real (6)
7. Fasten shut (4)
8. Ice cream is often served in one (4)
10. Stretch to breaking-point (6)
11. Wild, violent (6)

DOWN

2. These vegetables can make you cry (6)
3. Jars (4)
4. Island-nation in Northern Europe with many active volcanoes (7)
5. Too much (6)
6. Big Bird lives on _ _ _ _ _ _ Street (6)
9. Mount _ _ _ _ is an active volcano on the island of Sicily (4)

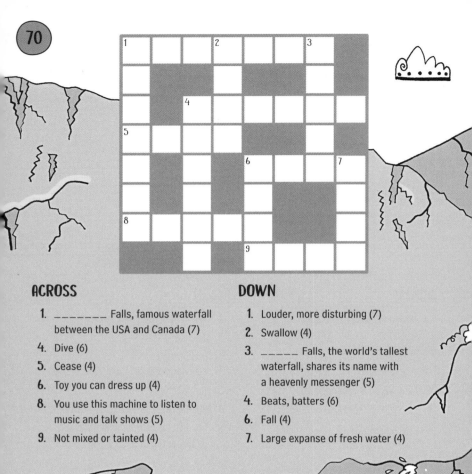

70

ACROSS

1. _____ Falls, famous waterfall between the USA and Canada (7)
4. Dive (6)
5. Cease (4)
6. Toy you can dress up (4)
8. You use this machine to listen to music and talk shows (5)
9. Not mixed or tainted (4)

DOWN

1. Louder, more disturbing (7)
2. Swallow (4)
3. _____ Falls, the world's tallest waterfall, shares its name with a heavenly messenger (5)
4. Beats, batters (6)
6. Fall (4)
7. Large expanse of fresh water (4)

ACROSS

1. _ _ _ _ _ _ _ _ Holmes overcame his arch-enemy Moriarty at Switzerland's Reichenbach Falls (8)
5. The Iguazu Falls lie between South America's largest countries, _ _ _ _ _ _ and Argentina (6)
7. Fruit peel (4)
8. Move by turning (4)
10. Calm down, relieve (6)
11. You use these for plucking hairs (8)

DOWN

1. Take away (8)
2. Internet letters (6)
3. Den, hideout (4)
4. Caring, helpfulness (8)
6. Small (6)
9. Strong affection (4)

ACROSS

1. Highest mountain in Wales (7)
5. Plant with a thin, climbing stem (4)
6. Wash briefly (5)
8. Practical art (5)
10. Seep (4)
11. Wild, rocky area in Devon with a famous old prison (8)

DOWN

1. English forest where Robin Hood is said to have lived (8)
2. It's used for roasting and baking (4)
3. The White Cliffs of _ _ _ _ _ lie on England's south coast (5)
4. "As light as a _ _ _ _ _ _ _" (7)
7. Perfume (5)
9. Combed-out, curly hairstyle (4)

ACROSS

1. Southwestern county of England famous for its pasties (8)
5. This river flows through London (6)
7. Floor of a ship (4)
8. Long periods of time (4)
10. Uncover (6)
11. Radiant (7)

DOWN

1. Little country houses (8)
2. Book user (6)
3. Plant growing where it's not wanted (4)
4. Fortunately (7)
6. The longest river in Great Britain, it flows from mid-Wales to the Bristol Channel (6)
9. "She looked like she'd _ _ _ _ a ghost!" (4)

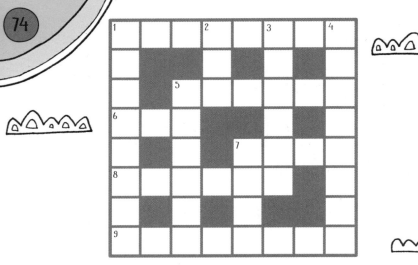

ACROSS

1. City in Nevada, USA, famed for its casinos (3, 5)
5. The Grand _ _ _ _ _ _ in Arizona is one of America's most famous landmarks (6)
6. How many wheels are there on a bicycle? (3)
7. In this place (4)
8. Stove (6)
9. Pullovers (8)

DOWN

1. Leafy salad vegetables (8)
2. Through (3)
3. Spring that spurts steam and hot water (6)
4. Light rays (8)
5. Wild American desert dog (6)
7. Warmth (4)

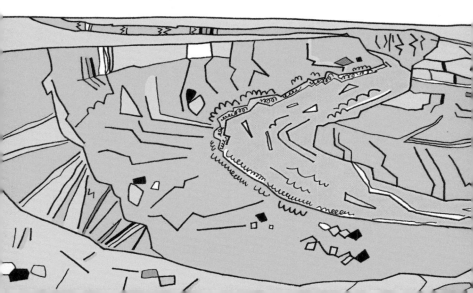

ACROSS

1. This US river flows from the state that shares its name down to Mexico (8)
5. Huge American vulture (6)
7. Rip (4)
8. Flying saucers (4)
10. Beginner (6)
11. Magnificent (8)

DOWN

1. Prickly desert plants (8)
2. John _ _ _ _ _ _ was a Beatle (6)
3. Public disorder (4)
4. Up above (8)
6. Jog someone's memory (6)
9. Tender, achey (4)

ACROSS

1. The largest of North America's Great Lakes, or a word meaning "better" (8)
5. Lake _ _ _ _ _ _ lies in the Alps between Switzerland and France (6)
7. An appeal for help (4)
8. Defrost (4)
10. Loch _ _ _ _ _ _ is Scotland's biggest lake (6)
11. Lazy, orange cartoon cat (8)

DOWN

1. A glimpse (8)
2. A friend you write to abroad (3, 3)
3. You write these letters at the end of an invitation (1.1.1.1.)
4. Paid, given a prize (8)
6. Nook, cubbyhole (6)
9. *The Boy Who Cried* _ _ _ _ is a story about why you shouldn't lie (4)

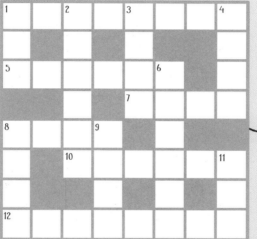

ACROSS

1. Gymnasts who perform tricks (8)

5. Hurried (6)

7. How many Great Lakes are there in North America? (4)

8. Food to attract fish (4)

10. Which legendary king was given a sword by the Lady of the Lake? (6)

12. Set free (8)

DOWN

1. You breathe it (3)

2. Large country where Lake Baikal, the world's deepest lake, is found (6)

3. Cow meat (4)

4. Certain (4)

6. Plates and bowls (6)

8. Great ____ Lake, the largest in Canada, is named for a wild animal (4)

9. A weeping willow is a type of what? (4)

11. Something misleading or distracting may be called a "___ herring" (3)

ACROSS

1. Africa or Asia, for example (9)
5. The central part of the Earth, or of an apple (4)
6. Got smaller (6)
9. Having dropped (6)
11. Clocks tell this (4)
12. The day before today (9)

DOWN

1. The outermost layer of the Earth, or of a loaf (5)
2. Close by (4)
3. The Earth's 5 across is made of the metals iron and _ _ _ _ _ _ (6)
4. Golfball stand (3)
7. Influence (6)
8. Tintin's little white dog (5)
10. Part of the Earth not covered by water (4)
11. Attempt (3)

ACROSS

1. Vitamin (7)
4. The Earth's surface is divided into slow-moving plates that fit together like a giant _ _ _ _ _ _ puzzle (6)
5. Pulse, rhythm (4)
7. Mash with your teeth (4)
11. It attracts metal (6)
12. Type of hard rock (7)

DOWN

1. Underground lava (5)
2. Tidy (4)
3. Opposite of asleep (5)
4. Task (3)
6. Go in (5)
8. Used to attach a door to its frame (5)
9. Damp (3)
10. Cab (4)

ACROSS

1. _ _ _ _ _ _ Island in the South Pacific is famous for its giant stone heads (6)
4. Casual denim clothes first sold by US businessman Levi Strauss (4, 5)
6. Pacific islands whose wildlife was studied by Charles Darwin (9)
8. They build bridges and machines (9)
10. Spoke, discussed (6)

DOWN

1. December 24th is Christmas _ _ _ (3)
2. Sound of a plucked string (5)
3. Opposes, stands up against (7)
4. The Pacific is the _ _ _ _ _ _ _ of all the world's oceans (7)
5. South Asian country, capital Tokyo (5)
7. Allowed by law (5)
9. Finale (3)

ACROSS

1. Large water bird with a huge beak (7)
5. Beneath (5)
6. Lip, edge (3)
8. National bird of New Zealand (4)
10. Plural of him or her (4)
12. Not bright (3)
13. Disney heroine who teams up with demigod Maui to save her people (5)
15. Information posters (7)

DOWN

1. Removed with a sharp tug (7)
2. Top, cover (3)
3. String (4)
4. New Zealand's _ _ _ _ _ Island is where most of its people live (5)
7. Animals that feed their young with milk (7)
9. Adult female (5)
11. Leave out (4)
14. Joan of _ _ _, French heroine (3)

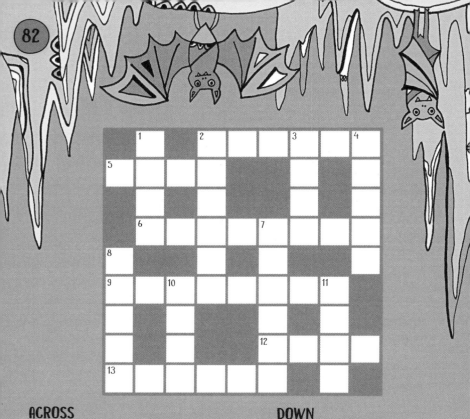

ACROSS

2. Something you know, but don't tell everyone (6)
5. Slightly wet (4)
6. Eagerness (8)
9. Light on a caver's or miner's helmet (8)
12. Flying animals that sleep upside-down (4)
13. Dark and cheerless (6)

DOWN

1. The opposite of light (4)
2. Open or stretch out (6)
3. A climber uses this (4)
4. Grilled bread (5)
7. Close (6)
8. Object, item (5)
10. As well (4)
11. Sympathy (4)

ACROSS

1. Wide-open (6)
5. Enclosed area in a building (4)
6. Caves are often made of this rock. Its name may remind you of a green citrus fruit (9)
9. Umbrella-shaped vegetables that grow in damp places (9)
12. Hollow, cavity (4)
13. Calm, peaceful (6)

DOWN

1. Bilbo Baggins took a magical ring from this cave-dwelling creature (6)
2. *Jabberwocky* is a _ _ _ _ by Lewis Carroll (4)
3. Cave, or somewhere you might see Santa (6)
4. In the near future (4)
7. Sounds that repeat and fade (6)
8. Make certain (6)
10. On top of (4)
11. Woodwind instrument (4)

ACROSS

1. This prickly plant with a fluffy, purple flower is a symbol of Scotland (7)
5. Answer (5)
7. Simon _ _ _ _, British comic actor who plays Scotty in the *Star Trek* movies (4)
9. This river on the Scottish-English border gives its name to a cloth (5)
10. The stories of the day (4)
11. Strong iron alloy (5)
13. Flow of vehicles (7)

DOWN

1. Traditional Scottish criss-cross pattern (6)
2. Sprite, goblin (3)
3. Something you play with (3)
4. Finished (5)
6. Rules (4)
7. Nuisance (4)
8. Celtic language spoken in Scotland (6)
9. Bird noise, or Twitter post (5)
11. Large area of salt water (3)
12. Pixie, fairy (3)

ACROSS

1. This Scottish mountain is the highest in Great Britain (3, 5)
5. Journalist (8)
7. Opposite of off (2)
8. The largest continent (4)
9. Deep, narrow mountain valley (4)
11. This Scottish lake is said to hide a famous monster (4, 4)
14. The Scottish _ _ _ _ _ _ _ _ Games includes caber tossing and bagpipe playing (8)

DOWN

1. Farm buildings (5)
2. Midday (4)
3. Essential, necessary (5)
4. Loud warning device on emergency vehicles (5)
6. Cook in hot but not boiling water (5)
8. Arabic word for God (5)
9. "_ _ _ whiz!" (3)
10. Became less difficult (5)
12. Toothed wheel inside a machine (3)
13. Zero points (3)

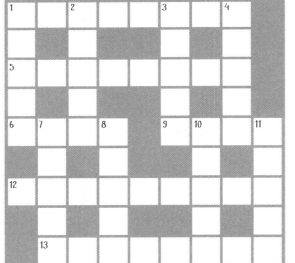

ACROSS

1. This eastern region of Canada gave its name to a breed of retriever dog (8)
5. Goodbye (8)
6. Edge (4)
9. Pulped potato (4)
12. Long, green salad vegetables (9)
13. Decorated wall hanging seen in castles (8)

DOWN

1. Raises (5)
2. Fed up (5)
3. Story in your head at night (5)
4. Buns (5)
7. Native people of Arctic Canada (5)
8. Supply, prepare (5)
10. Wide awake (5)
11. Sled-dog (5)

ACROSS

1. Main language in Québec, Canada (6)
4. Opposite of wild (4)
6. Highway (4)
7. Slang for "lots" (6)
9. Funeral casket (6)
12. Region (4)
13. Require (4)
14. Entertained (6)

DOWN

1. Sense (4)
2. You use them to hear (4)
3. _ _ _ _ _ _ Bay, huge Canadian bay (6)
5. *Much _ _ _ about Nothing*, Shakespeare play (3)
7. Capital of Canada (6)
8. Self-importance (3)
9. Popular pets (4)
10. Discover (4)
11. Frozen water (3)

ACROSS

1. Provence in southern France is famous for growing this scented purple flower (8)
5. Uses a chair (4)
7. Spanish city famous for its oranges (7)
9. Countries (7)
12. Alone (4)
13. Great worry or pain (8)

DOWN

1. Capital of Portugal (6)
2. Tanks, large containers (4)
3. Plans to make something (7)
4. Safety bar (4)
6. Important, solemn (7)
8. Mistakes (6)
10. Grew older (4)
11. An amount (4)

ACROSS

1. Big city on Spain's northeast coast with a famous soccer team (9)
5. Piece of music with words (4)
7. Bigger or more important (7)
9. Less old (7)
12. Mound of sand built by wind (4)
13. Top news stories (9)

DOWN

1. The Bay of _ _ _ _ _ _ lies between France and Spain (6)
2. It's worn on a finger (4)
3. Found (7)
4. Big city on France's southeast coat, or a word meaning "pleasant" (4)
6. Smiled broadly (7)
8. The Rhône and Loire are French _ _ _ _ _ _ (6)
10. A single time (4)
11. Crumbling building (4)

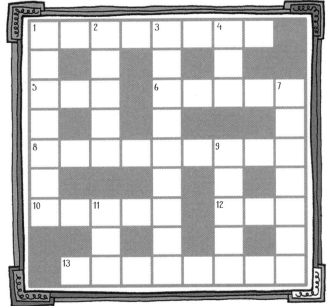

ACROSS

1. Explorer Christopher _____ reached the Americas in 1492 (8)
5. Cut grass (3)
6. Sir Francis _____ sailed around the world in the *Golden Hind* (5)
8. James Cook reached _____ in 1770 (9)
10. Japanese rice rolls (5)
12. Short for Melanie (3)
13. Worried and exhausted from having to cope with too much (8)

DOWN

1. Direction-finding tool (7)
2. _____ and Clark explored and mapped America in the 1800s (5)
3. Bring up to date (9)
4. America (1.1.1.)
7. Made possible (7)
9. James Cook fed these citrus fruits to his crew to keep them healthy (5)
11. Group of things that go together (3)

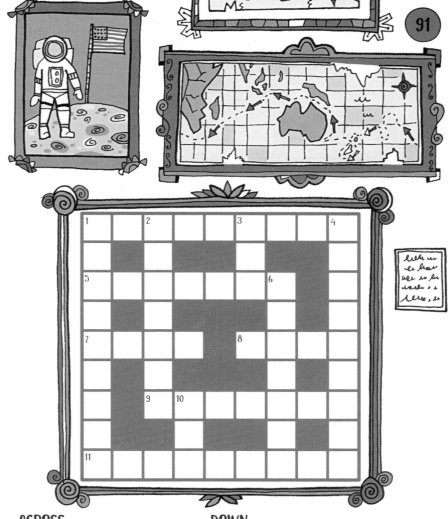

ACROSS

1. He explored medieval China (5, 4)
5. Giving a short cry of pain (7)
7. "The hen _ _ _ _ an egg" (4)
8. "_ _ _ _! Wanna hear a secret?" (4)
9. Sir Edmund _ _ _ _ _ _ _ was the first to climb Everest, with Tenzing Norgay (7)
11. Raided, turned inside-out (9)

DOWN

1. Ship that carried the Pilgrim Fathers to America in 1620 (9)
2. Sir Walter _ _ _ _ _ _ _ searched South America for the legendary City of Gold (7)
3. Peter _ _ _, Wendy's flying friend (3)
4. If you've "_ _ _ _ _ _ _ _ your welcome" then it's time to leave (9)
6. It protects you from dangerous fumes (3, 4)
10. "The _ _ _ and outs" are the details (3)

ACROSS

1. Large country north of China, homeland of Genghis Khan (8)
5. Opposite of false (4)
6. Two plus two _ _ _ _ _ _ four (6)
8. Attached with metal spikes (6)
10. Metal (4)
11. In a flash (8)

DOWN

1. Glove without separate fingers (6)
2. Large Arctic island-nation between Canada and Iceland (9)
3. Mash into a fluid (9)
4. Absent without leave (1.1.1.1.)
7. Thin (6)
9. Upper limbs (4)

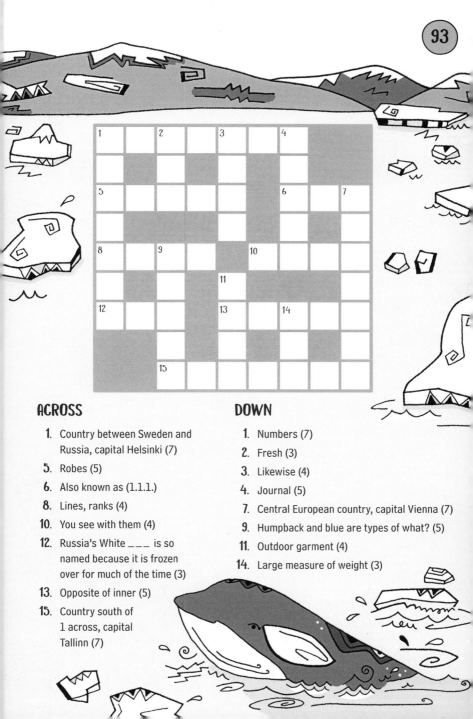

ACROSS

1. Country between Sweden and Russia, capital Helsinki (7)

5. Robes (5)

6. Also known as (1.1.1.)

8. Lines, ranks (4)

10. You see with them (4)

12. Russia's White ___ is so named because it is frozen over for much of the time (3)

13. Opposite of inner (5)

15. Country south of 1 across, capital Tallinn (7)

DOWN

1. Numbers (7)

2. Fresh (3)

3. Likewise (4)

4. Journal (5)

7. Central European country, capital Vienna (7)

9. Humpback and blue are types of what? (5)

11. Outdoor garment (4)

14. Large measure of weight (3)

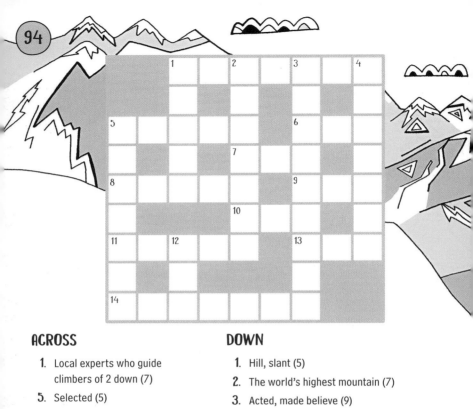

ACROSS

1. Local experts who guide climbers of 2 down (7)
5. Selected (5)
6. Very long period, age (3)
7. Furrow, groove (3)
8. Section, part (5)
9. Ostrich-like Australian bird (3)
10. Male child (3)
11. Region of China by 2 down (5)
13. Short for Daniel (3)
14. Snow _ _ _ _ _ _ _, a spotted big cat (7)

DOWN

1. Hill, slant (5)
2. The world's highest mountain (7)
3. Acted, made believe (9)
4. Perhaps surprisingly, you need cream to prevent this in snowy mountain areas (7)
5. A country's or region's main city (7)
12. If you like it, you clap, if you hate it, you _ _ _ (3)

ACROSS

1. New _ _ _ _ _, India's capital (5)
4. Beginning (5, 4)
6. School test (4)
7. Legendary ape-like creature said to live in the 8 across (4)
8. This Asian mountain range is home to the world's highest mountain (9)
10. Country in the 8 across (5)

DOWN

1. Romantic outing (4)
2. Raffle (7)
3. Hints at, suggests (7)
4. Spruce up, revive (7)
5. Useful aid for drivers (4, 3)
9. Laugh out loud (1.1.1.)

ACROSS

1. Yellow, trumpet-shaped flower (8)
6. A or E, for example (5)
7. Star sign of the Lion (3)
8. Tall, scented flower (4)
10. Great in length (4)
12. Move into place, position (3)
13. Exceed, go one better (5)
15. Put together, construct (8)

DOWN

1. Grows, matures (8)
2. Not many (3)
3. Night birds (4)
4. Dome built out of snow or ice (5)
5. Tall, showy plant with with drooping, purplish-pink bell-shaped flowers (8)
9. Type of water lily (5)
11. Scented flower with thorns (4)
14. "Rub-a-dub-dub, three men in a _ _ _" (3)

ACROSS

1. Bluish-purple shade named for a wild pansy (6)
4. Adds sugar (8)
7. Giant plant with a big, round, yellow-petalled head filled with dark seeds (9)
11. Shared feeling, pity (8)
13. Make a small hole in (6)

DOWN

1. Flower jars (5)
2. The Atlantic, for example (5)
3. Fasten (3)
5. Cup-shaped garden flower (5)
6. To "___ red" is to fly into a rage (3)
8. "Life is full of ___ and downs" (3)
9. You _____ plants to keep them alive (5)
10. "Flower" and "power" do this (5)
12. You use it to wash the floor (3)

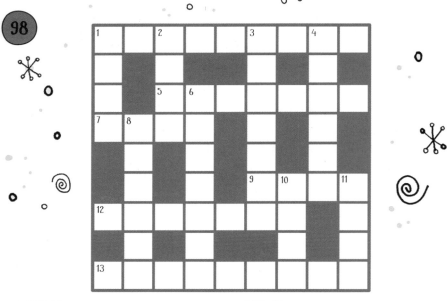

ACROSS

1. Large, meat-eating wild animal that lives around the North Pole (5, 4)
5. Crush, crumple up (7)
7. Alongside (4)
9. Every (4)
12. Frozen block floating in the sea (7)
13. Got smaller (9)

DOWN

1. Front of a boat (4)
2. Off-track, missing (4)
3. Whale fat (7)
4. Region around the North Pole (6)
6. Room (7)
8. Frozen drip (6)
10. "I haven't seen you in ____!" (4)
11. Difficult (4)

ACROSS

1. North American reindeer (7)
6. His workshop is at the North Pole (5)
7. Money given to the government to pay for things like roads and schools (3)
8. Killer whale (4)
10. Sea mammal with whiskers (4)
12. One of 6 across's little helpers (3)
13. First name shared by writer Dahl and polar explorer Amundsen (5)
15. Alarmed, surprised (7)

DOWN

1. Client (8)
2. Drip rapidly, flow (3)
3. Small sea vessel (4)
4. Loosen a knot (5)
5. Blew up (8)
9. Coffee shops (5)
11. Group of three people (4)
14. Request (3)

ACROSS

1. Big city in Tennessee, USA, on the shores of the Mississippi River (7)
5. Difficult test (9)
6. A flower, or part of the eye (4)
7. It goes with a knife (4)
10. Crocodile relative found in the Florida Everglades (9)
12. Resists, fights against (7)

DOWN

1. Big city on the south Florida coast (5)
2. It comes from cows (4)
3. ___ Solo, *Star Wars* hero (3)
4. Casual sports shoe (7)
5. Big US city with a musical named after it (7)
8. Vows (5)
9. "Don't put all your ____ in one basket" (4)
11. Cut off a twig or branch (3)

ACROSS

1. The northeastern tip of the USA is known as New _ _ _ _ _ _ _ (7)
5. America's top elected leader (9)
7. Slang for "isn't", "aren't" and "am not" (4)
8. Opposite of good (4)
11. Capital of Tennessee, home of American country music (9)
13. Snake (7)

DOWN

1. Spell out, make clear (7)
2. A _ _ _ _ _ light means "go" (5)
3. Enthusiastic, passionate (4)
4. Expected to arrive (3)
6. Highest (7)
9. Worth (5)
10. At any time (4)
12. Distress call (1.1.1.)

ACROSS

1. Pottery, ceramics (5)
4. The mother of a marriage partner is called a mother-__-___ (2-3)
7. Rockfall (9)
8. Previous (5)
9. Large deer (3)
10. Instance, illustration (7)
11. Cease to live (3)

DOWN

1. Fall down, crumble (8)
2. Exactly the same (9)
3. Runways (9)
5. Hung around (8)
6. Rubble, debris (8)

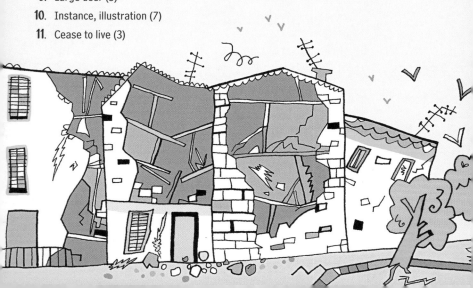

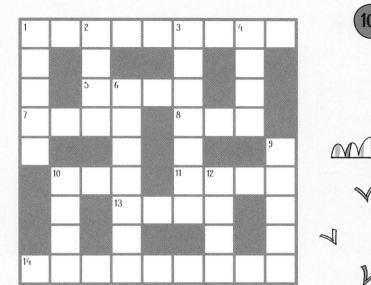

ACROSS

1. San _ _ _ _ _ _ _ _ _, big Californian city devastated by an earthquake in 1906 (9)
5. Tiny particle making up all things (4)
7. Sets down (4)
8. Female sheep (3)
10. Cooling device (3)
11. Move from side to side (4)
13. Vicinity (4)
14. Healing drugs (9)

DOWN

1. Responsibility for a wrong (5)
2. Absent (4)
3. Vast (7)
4. Remedy (4)
6. Giant wave caused by a seaquake (7)
9. Ancient tales of gods and heroes (5)
10. The Ring of _ _ _ _ is a volcanic zone around the Pacific Ocean (4)
12. Alert others to danger (4)

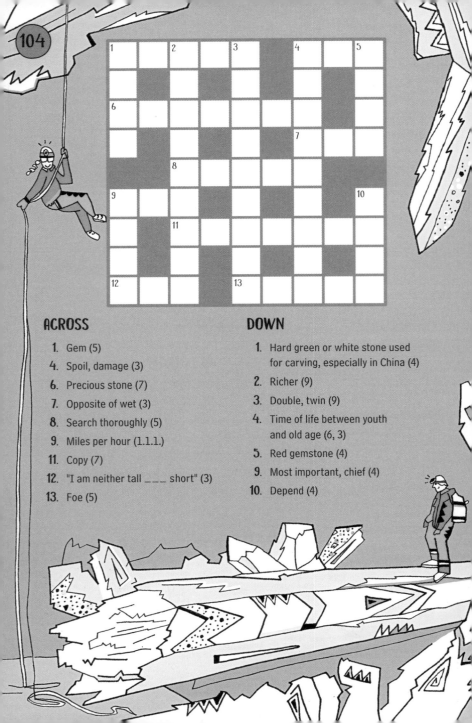

ACROSS

1. Gem (5)
4. Spoil, damage (3)
6. Precious stone (7)
7. Opposite of wet (3)
8. Search thoroughly (5)
9. Miles per hour (1.1.1.)
11. Copy (7)
12. "I am neither tall ___ short" (3)
13. Foe (5)

DOWN

1. Hard green or white stone used for carving, especially in China (4)
2. Richer (9)
3. Double, twin (9)
4. Time of life between youth and old age (6, 3)
5. Red gemstone (4)
9. Most important, chief (4)
10. Depend (4)

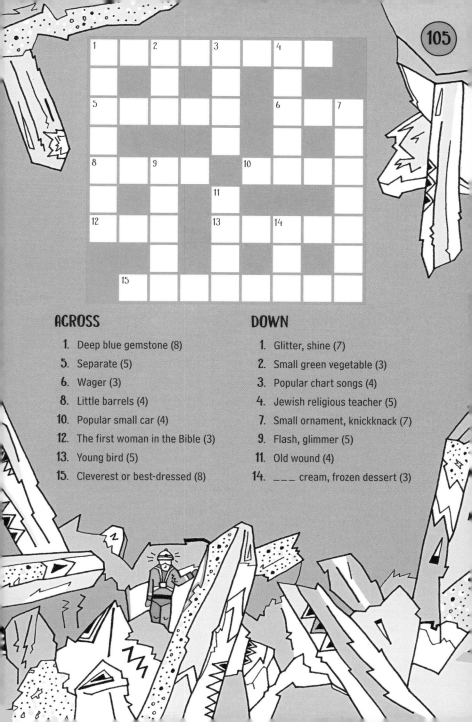

ACROSS

1. Deep blue gemstone (8)
5. Separate (5)
6. Wager (3)
8. Little barrels (4)
10. Popular small car (4)
12. The first woman in the Bible (3)
13. Young bird (5)
15. Cleverest or best-dressed (8)

DOWN

1. Glitter, shine (7)
2. Small green vegetable (3)
3. Popular chart songs (4)
4. Jewish religious teacher (5)
7. Small ornament, knickknack (7)
9. Flash, glimmer (5)
11. Old wound (4)
14. ___ cream, frozen dessert (3)

ACROSS

1. Guide a ship or plane using a map (8)
5. Problem, hitch (4)
6. Fly high (4)
7. Turn up to a party uninvited (9)
11. Spheres (4)
12. Entrance (4)
13. EU stands for _ _ _ _ _ _ _ _ Union (8)

DOWN

1. Black-clad Japanese assassin (5)
2. Unclear (5)
3. Hawaiian greeting (5)
4. Our planet (5)
7. A model of 4 down (5)
8. Rome's river (5)
9. Raised strip (5)
10. The dish ran away with the what? (5)

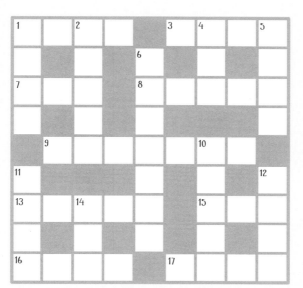

ACROSS

1. Young sheep (4)
3. On pirate maps, X marks the _ _ _ _ (4)
7. Guide to a map's symbols (3)
8. Small measure of weight (5)
9. There are 360 in a circle (7)
13. Chain of mountains (5)
15. Unwell (3)
16. Responsibility (4)
17. Opposite of east (4)

DOWN

1. Similar to (4)
2. Perhaps (5)
4. Fastener (3)
5. Long hike (4)
6. Trip (7)
10. Banishment (5)
11. Crossed lines that make squares on a map (4)
12. Storyline (4)
14. A pecan is a what? (3)

ACROSS

1. You put them on birthday cakes (7)
4. All the Scandinavian countries have lands inside the Arctic _ _ _ _ _ _ (6)
7. A blacksmith hammers upon it (5)
9. Elegance, flair (5)
11. Sharp, shrewd (6)
12. This Danish prince is the lead character of Shakespeare's most famous play (6)

DOWN

1. Bike-rider (7)
2. Scandinavian country famous for its many fjords (6)
3. Opposite of odd (4)
5. Finland is known as the Land of a Thousand _ _ _ _ _ (5)
6. Nearest (7)
8. Having to do with sight (6)
10. Whip (4)

ACROSS

1. In Scandinavian legends, ugly creatures that live in lonely places (6)
5. The Norse god of thunder (4)
6. Long, tiring work (4)
8. Short-lived wild flowers with fragile petals (7)
11. The southernmost Scandinavian country, capital Copenhagen (7)
15. Norway's capital (4)
16. Hold firmly (4)
17. The largest Scandinavian country, capital Stockholm (6)

DOWN

1. Threw, flipped (6)
2. Danish toy company famed for its plastic bricks (4)
3. Prevent (4)
4. A dog might chew it (4)
7. Not closed (4)
9. Irritates (4)
10. Wild West bar (6)
12. Noble rank (4)
13. Navigation aids (4)
14. Roam, wander (4)

ACROSS

1. The River Amazon winds through the South American rain_____ (6)
4. Big South American country, capital Buenos Aires (9)
6. Grasp (4)
8. Pig fat (4)
10. Comic-book character who uses special powers to fight crime (9)
11. Precious green stone (7)

DOWN

1. Gives off bursts of light (7)
2. Royal, majestic (5)
3. Final sum (5)
5. Robot, or a type of smartphone (7)
7. Imagine, fantasize (5)
9. Stadium (5)

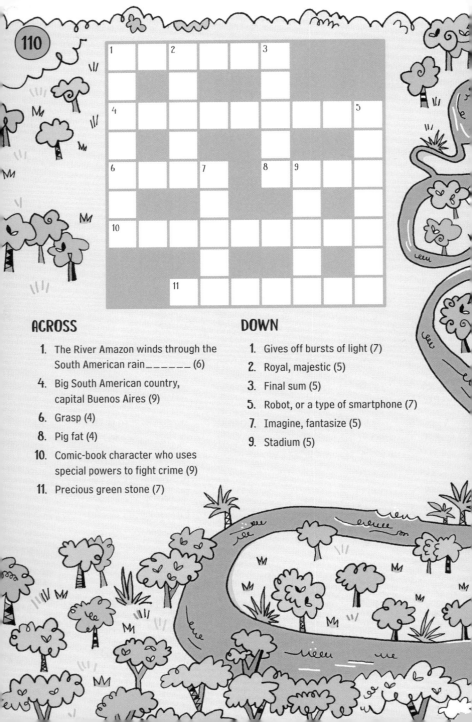

ACROSS

1. South American nation, capital Bogotá (8)
5. Cry of insight or discovery (3)
6. Belonging to you (5)
8. Frog-like creature (4)
9. Which civilization built Machu Picchu? (4)
12. Long, thin country on South America's west coast (5)
14. ___-Wan Kenobi, Jedi knight (3)
15. Thrive (8)

DOWN

1. Wild, disorganized (7)
2. Thick-coated pack animal that lives in the Andes Mountains (5)
3. Ancient Central American people (4)
4. Record of a debt (1.1.1.)
7. Most South American countries speak this language (7)
10. _____ Campbell, British model (5)
11. South American country, capital Lima (4)
13. Short for "I will" (3)

ACROSS

1. Robert Falcon _ _ _ _ _ led an expedition to the South Pole in 1910 (5)
4. Young goat (3)
6. "Walking _ _ _ _ _ _ _ _ _" means the same as "playing with fire" (2,4,3)
7. Uses a needle and thread (4)
9. "Four _ _ _ _ five equals nine" (4)
12. Region around the South Pole (9)
14. Automobile (3)
15. The 12 across has the fastest _ _ _ _ _ on Earth (5)

DOWN

1. Surprisingly, it rarely _ _ _ _ _ in the 12 across (5)
2. Not at home (3)
3. Journey (4)
4. Swarming shrimp-like creatures (5)
5. Stain, pigment (3)
8. 70% of the world's fresh _ _ _ _ _ is held in the ice of the 12 across (5)
10. They keep your feet warm (5)
11. Team that runs a ship (4)
12. Alphabet (1.1.1.)
13. Metal (3)

ACROSS

1. In-depth study (8)
5. Trembled with cold or fear (8)
7. Opposite of float (4)
8. Hair-grooming tool (4)
11. Flightless black-and-white birds that live around the South Pole (8)
12. Gifts (8)

DOWN

1. Dangers (5)
2. Chemistry and physics are both types of this (7)
3. Mountaineers and polar explorers use ice _ _ _ _ to help them climb (4)
4. Did have (3)
6. Feeling (7)
9. Command posts, headquarters (5)
10. Birds lay them (4)
11. Young seal (3)

114

ACROSS

1. A nature _ _ _ _ _ _ _ is a place where wildlife is protected (7)
5. Slang for police officer (3)
6. Divide up and hand out (5)
8. Be concerned about others (4)
9. Tight fastening in string or rope (4)
12. In addition, over and above (5)
14. Forbid, make illegal (3)
15. Stop from happening (7)

DOWN

1. Turn waste into new things (7)
2. Fantastic, brilliant (5)
3. The _ _ _ _ is the remaining part (4)
4. Girl's name (3)
7. Died out, gone forever (7)
10. Principled, admirable (5)
11. Rescue (4)
13. Upper part (3)

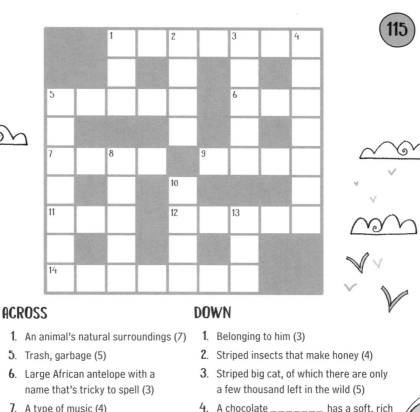

ACROSS

1. An animal's natural surroundings (7)
5. Trash, garbage (5)
6. Large African antelope with a name that's tricky to spell (3)
7. A type of music (4)
9. Short for professor (4)
11. 5 down is melting the _ _ _ at the Earth's Poles (3)
12. The _ _ _ _ _ layer protects the Earth from harmful rays (5)
14. Real, authentic (7)

DOWN

1. Belonging to him (3)
2. Striped insects that make honey (4)
3. Striped big cat, of which there are only a few thousand left in the wild (5)
4. A chocolate _ _ _ _ _ _ _ has a soft, rich filling and usually a rounded shape (7)
5. Global _ _ _ _ _ _ _ is the increase in worldwide temperatures (7)
8. _ _ _ _ _ energy is energy that does not create pollution or toxic waste (5)
10. Picnic-pilfering cartoon bear (4)
13. How many planets do we know for sure have life on them? (3)

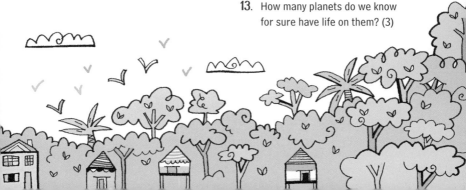

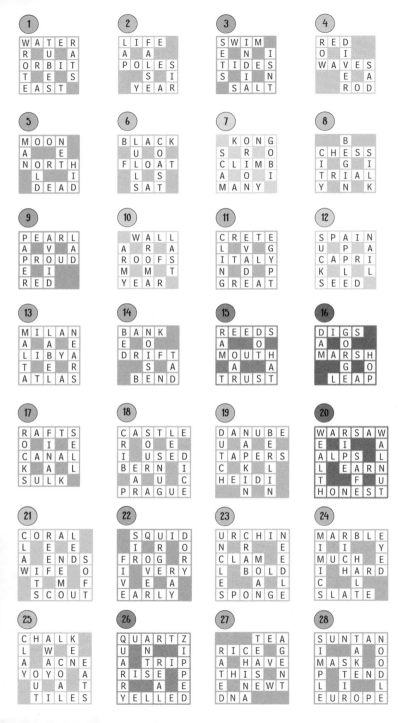

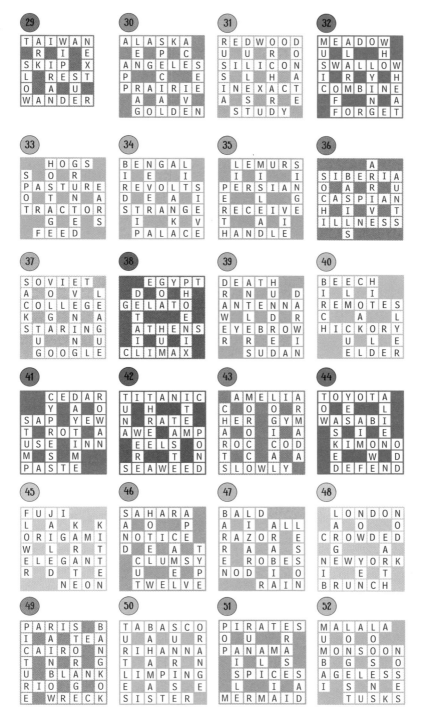

29
```
T A I W A N
. R . I . E
S K I P . X
L . R E S T
O . A . U .
W A N D E R
```

30
```
A L A S K A
. E . P . C
A N G E L E S
P . C . . E
P R A I R I E
. A . A . V
G O L D E N
```

31
```
R E D W O O D
U . U . R . O
S I L I C O N
S . L . H . A
I N E X A C T
A . S . R . E
. S T U D Y
```

32
```
M E A D O W
U . L . . H
S W A L L O W
I . R . Y . H
C O M B I N E
. F . . N . A
F O R G E T
```

33
```
. H O G S
S . O . R
P A S T U R E
O . T . N . A
T R A C T O R
. G . E . S
F E E D
```

34
```
B E N G A L
I . E . . I
R E V O L T S
D . E . A . T
S T R A N G E
. I . K . V
P A L A C E
```

35
```
L E M U R S
. I . I . I
P E R S I A N
E . L . . G
R E C E I V E
T . A . I .
H A N D L E
```

36
```
. . . . A
S I B E R I A
O . A . R . U
C A S P I A N
H . I . V . T
I L L N E S S
. . . S
```

37
```
S O V I E T
A . O . V . L
C O L L E G E
K . G . N . A
S T A R I N G
. U . N . U
G O O G L E
```

38
```
. E G Y P T
. D . O . H
G E L A T O
. T . . E
. A T H E N S
. I . U . I
C L I M A X
```

39
```
D E A T H
R . N . U . D
A N T E N N A
W . L . D . R
E Y E B R O W
R . R . E . I
. S U D A N
```

40
```
B E E C H
I . L . I
R E M O T E S
C . A . L
H I C K O R Y
. U . L . E
E L D E R
```

41
```
. C E D A R
. Y . A . O
S A P . Y E W
T . R O T . A
U S E . I N N
M . S . M
P A S T E
```

42
```
T I T A N I C
U . H . . T
N . R A T E
A W E . A M P
. E E L S . O
. R . . T . N
S E A W E E D
```

43
```
. A M E L I A
C . O . O . R
H E R . G Y M
A . O . I . A
R O C . C O D
T . C . A . A
S L O W L Y
```

44
```
T O Y O T A
O . E . . L
W A S A B I
. S . I . E
K I M O N O
E . . W . D
D E F E N D
```

45
```
F U J I
L . A . K . K
O R I G A M I
W . L . R . T
E L E G A N T
R . D . T . E
. N E O N
```

46
```
S A H A R A
A . O . . P
N O T I C E
D . E . A . T
. C L U M S Y
. U . E . P
T W E L V E
```

47
```
B A L D
A . I . A L L
R A Z O R . E
R . A . S .
E . R O B E S
N O D . I . O
. . R A I N
```

48
```
. L O N D O N
A . O . . O
C R O W D E D
G . . . A
N E W Y O R K
I . . E . T
B R U N C H
```

49
```
P A R I S . B
I . A . T E A
C A I R O . N
T . N . R . G
U . B L A N K
R I O . G . O
E . W R E C K
```

50
```
T A B A S C O
U . A . U . R
R I H A N N A
T . A . R . N
L I M P I N G
E . A . S . E
S I S T E R
```

51
```
P I R A T E S
O . U . . R
P A N A M A
. I . L . S
S P I C E S
. L . I . A
M E R M A I D
```

52
```
M A L A L A
U . O . O
M O N S O O N
B . G . S . O
A G E L E S S
I . S . N . E
. T U S K S
```

53

```
M A H A T M A
U   I   R
G A N G E S
S   D   A   L
  J U N G L E
  O       E   G
I G N O R E S
```

54

```
M O L E S
O   E   P I T
M I N E R   H
E   D   I   O
N   I N N E R
T E N   G   N
    G A S P S
```

55

```
C A B L E
A   R   A S H
R O O T S   A
R   W   T   M
O   S L E E P
T I E   R   E
    S O N A R
```

56

```
O U T B A C K
  L   A     I
H U R R I E D
  R   R   D
O U T I N G S
P   E   E
T O U R I S T
```

57

```
  K O A L A
  N   L   R
V I S I T E D
  F   C   N
R E P E A T S
A   E   L   E
M A T I L D A
```

58

```
B L I Z Z A R D
R   D   O     R
A   E   N E R O
C R A T E     U
E     U S I N G
L E A N   D   H
E     E   L   T
T W I S T E R
```

59

```
T Y P H O O N
O   O   U     T
R   W A R M T H
N O D   A   U
A   E   S U N
D I R E C T   D
O     E   E   E
  D E A R E R
```

60

```
B I G F O O T
E   O   W   A
R E I G N   L
R   N   S T E M
Y O G A   R   A
  P   B L A C K
  E   L   I   E
  N E E D L E S
```

61

```
  S A P L I N G
  H   E   K   L
  A G E   E   E
  D   P L A C E
D E N S E   O
U   U   D E N
E   T   G   E
L I S T E N S
```

62

```
F A I T H F U L
E   S   E     E
B I S O N     A
R   U   S E A R
U S E S   A   N
A     L O G O S
R     I   L
Y I P P E E
```

63

```
G R I Z Z L Y
I   E   A
A     S C R E W
N E S T   G   O
T   T   D E A L
S C E N E     V
    A   E     E
  I M P R E S S
```

64

```
A S T E R O I D
C   U   A     I
H O R N S     N
I   N   H E R O
E L S E   X   S
V     D R A M A
E     G   C   U
D I R E C T O R
```

65

```
F O S S I L S
L   T     A
I R O N I N G
N   N     D O T
T O E     M   E
  V A M P I R E
  E G     N   T
  R E F R E S H
```

66

```
E T H I O P I A
L     D   R   L
E   H O P I N G
C O O L   S   E
T   T   H O U R
I N D I A N   I
O     O   I   A
N I G E R I A
```

67

```
V I C T O R I A
E   U   V     C
T A S T E S   H
    T   R A C E
G L O W   F
O   M E T A L S
L     E   R   A
D O L P H I N S
```

68

```
V E S U V I U S
I   E   I     U
C R A T E R   R
T   R   W A R P
I N C H   V   R
M   H A W A I I
S     R   G   S
  C O M P E T E
```

69
```
. P O M P E I I
. N . O . . C .
E X I S T S . E
X . O . S E A L
C O N E . S . A
E . S T R A I N
S . . N . M . D
S A V A G E . .
```

70
```
N I A G A R A .
O . . U . . N .
I . P L U N G E
S T O P . . E .
I . U . D O L L
E . N . R . A .
R A D I O . K .
. . S . P U R E
```

71
```
S H E R L O C K
U . M . A . . I
B R A Z I L . N
T . I . R I N D
R O L L . T . N
A . S O O T H E
C . . . V . L S
T W E E Z E R S
```

72
```
S N O W D O N .
H . V . O . . F
E . E . V I N E
R I N S E . . A
W . . C R A F T
O O Z E . F . H
O . . N . R . E
D A R T M O O R
```

73
```
C O R N W A L L
O . E . E . . U
T H A M E S . C
T . D . D E C K
A G E S . V . I
G . R E V E A L
E . . E . R . Y
S H I N I N G .
```

74
```
L A S V E G A S
E . . I . E . U
T . C A N Y O N
T W O . . S . B
U . Y . H E R E
C O O K E R . A
E . T . A . . M
S W E A T E R S
```

75
```
C O L O R A D O
A . E . I . . V
C O N D O R . E
T . N . T E A R
U F O S . M . H
S . N O V I C E
E . . R . N . A
S P L E N D I D
```

76
```
S U P E R I O R
I . E . S . . E
G E N E V A . W
H . P . P L E A
T H A W . C . R
I . L O M O N D
N . . L . V . E
G A R F I E L D
```

77
```
A C R O B A T S
I . U . E . . U
R U S H E D . R
. . S . F I V E
B A I T . S . .
E . A R T H U R
A . E . E . E .
R E L E A S E D
```

78
```
C O N T I N E N T
R . E . I . . . E
U . A . C O R E .
S H R A N K . . .
T . F . E . . . S
. . F A L L E N .
T I M E . . A . O
R . C . . N . W
Y E S T E R D A Y
```

79
```
. M I N E R A L
. A . E . . W .
J I G S A W . A
O . M . T . K .
B E A T . C H E W
N . . T . I . E
T . M A G N E T
E . . X . G . .
G R A N I T E .
```

80
```
. . . E A S T E R
. . . V . W . . E
B L U E J E A N S
I . . A . N . . I
G A L A P A G O S
G . E . A . . . T
E N G I N E E R S
S . A . . N . . .
T A L K E D . . .
```

81
```
P E L I C A N .
L . I . O . O .
U N D E R . R I M
C . . D . T . A
K I W I . T H E M
E . O . O . . M
D I M . M O A N A
. A . I . R . L
. N O T I C E S
```

82
```
. D . S E C R E T
D A M P . O . O .
. R . R . P . A .
. K E E N N E S S
T . A . E . . T .
H E A D L A M P .
I . L . R . I .
N . S . . B A T S
G L O O M Y . Y .
```

83
```
G A P I N G . S .
O . O . . R O O M
L . E . . O . O .
L I M E S T O N E
U . C . T . . N .
M U S H R O O M S
. P . O . B . U .
H O L E . O . R .
. N . S E R E N E
```

84

```
T H I S T L E
A   M   O   N
R E P L Y   D
T   A   P E G G
A   T W E E D   A
N E W S   S   E
  E   S T E E L
  E   E   L   I
  T R A F F I C
```

85

```
B E N N E V I S
A   O   I   I
R E P O R T E R
N   O N   A   E
A S I A   G L E N
L   C   E   A
L O C H N E S S
A   O   I   E
H I G H L A N D
```

86

```
L A B R A D O R
I   O   R   O
F A R E W E L L
T   E   A   L
S I D E   M A S H
  N   Q   L   U
C U C U M B E R S
  I   I   R   K
T A P E S T R Y
```

87

```
    F R E N C H
T A M E   A   U
  D   E   R O A D
O O D L E S   S
T     G     O
T   C O F F I N
A R E A   I   C
W     T   N E E D
A M U S E D
```

88

```
L A V E N D E R
I   A   E   A
S I T S   S   I
B   S E V I L L E
O     R   G   R
N A T I O N S   R
  G   O   S O L O
  E   U   M   R
D I S T R E S S
```

89

```
B A R C E L O N A
I   I   O     I
S O N G   C   C
C   G R E A T E R
A     I   T   I
Y O U N G E R   V
  N   N   D U N E
  C   E     I   R
H E A D L I N E S
```

90

```
C O L U M B U S
O   E   O   S
M O W   D R A K E
P   I   E     N
A U S T R A L I A
S     N   I   B
S U S H I   M E L
  E   Z   E   E
S T R E S S E D
```

91

```
M A R C O P O L O
A   A   A     U
Y E L P I N G   T
F   E   A   S
L A I D   P S S T
O   G   M   A
W   H I L L A R Y
E   N   S   E
R A N S A C K E D
```

92

```
M O N G O L I A
I   R   I   W
T R U E   Q   O
T   E Q U A L S
E   N   I   K
N A I L E D   I
R   A   I R O N
M   N   Z   N
S U D D E N L Y
```

93

```
F I N L A N D
I   E   L   I
G O W N S   A K A
U   O   R   U
R O W S   E Y E S
E   H   C   T
S E A   O U T E R
  L   A   O   I
  E S T O N I A
```

94

```
  S H E R P A S
  L   V   R   U
C H O S E   E O N
A   P   R U T   B
P I E C E   E M U
I     S O N   R
T I B E T   D A N
A   O       E
L E O P A R D
```

95

```
      D E L H I
      A   O   M
F I R S T S T E P
R   O   E   T   L
E X A M   Y E T I
S   D     R   E
H I M A L A Y A S
E   A   O
N E P A L
```